THE SUN & MOON SIGNS LIBRARY

SAGITTARIUS

23 NOVEMBER – 21 DECEMBER

JULIA AND DEREK PARKER

Photography by Monique le Luhandre
Illustrations by Danuta Mayer

DK

DORLING KINDERSLEY
London · New York · Stuttgart

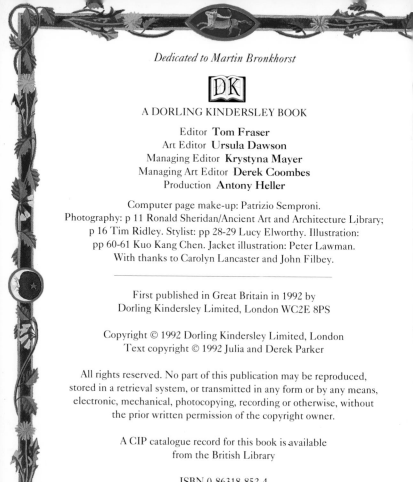

Dedicated to Martin Bronkhorst

DK

A DORLING KINDERSLEY BOOK

Editor **Tom Fraser**
Art Editor **Ursula Dawson**
Managing Editor **Krystyna Mayer**
Managing Art Editor **Derek Coombes**
Production **Antony Heller**

Computer page make-up: Patrizio Semproni.
Photography: p 11 Ronald Sheridan/Ancient Art and Architecture Library;
p 16 Tim Ridley. Stylist: pp 28-29 Lucy Elworthy. Illustration:
pp 60-61 Kuo Kang Chen. Jacket illustration: Peter Lawman.
With thanks to Carolyn Lancaster and John Filbey.

First published in Great Britain in 1992 by
Dorling Kindersley Limited, London WC2E 8PS

A CIP catalogue record for this book is available
from the British Library

ISBN 0-86318-852-4

Reproduced by GRB Editrice, Verona, Italy
Printed and bound in Hong Kong by Imago

CONTENTS

INTRODUCING
SAGITTARIUS

SAGITTARIUS, THE SIGN OF THE CENTAUR, THE ARCHER WHO IS
HALF MAN AND HALF BEAST, IS THE NINTH SIGN OF THE
ZODIAC. YOU NEED DEMANDING PHYSICAL OR INTELLECTUAL
EXERCISE IN ORDER TO FULFILL YOUR POTENTIAL.

Being a Sagittarian, you should guard against restlessness, and develop a sense of purpose. This will ensure that you possess the continuity of effort required for a full expression of your potential, and thus your psychological fulfilment.

You are likely to be one of the explorers and travellers of the Zodiac – both in mind and in body. You are willing to take risks, but must control a gambling spirit that can occasionally get out of hand.

Traditional groupings

As you read through this book you will come across references to the elements and the qualities, and to positive and negative, or masculine and feminine signs.

The first of these groupings, that of the elements, comprises fire, earth, air, and water signs. The second, that of the qualities, divides the Zodiac into cardinal, fixed, and mutable signs. The final grouping is made up of positive and negative, or masculine and feminine signs. Each Zodiac sign is associated with a combination of components from these groupings, all of which contribute different characteristics to it.

Sagittarian characteristics

Being a sign of the fire element, Sagittarius bestows great natural enthusiasm upon its subjects. This often extends to a fondness for demanding physical or intellectual exercise. Since Sagittarius is also a positive, masculine sign, you are liable to be one of the optimistic extroverts of the Zodiac. Being of the mutable quality, Sagittarius is a "dual" sign, and its subjects are therefore versatile.

The ruling planet of Sagittarius is Jupiter, the giant of the Solar System, and a great god in Roman mythology. The Sagittarian colours are rich purples and dark blues.

ARIES · PISCES · TAURUS · AQUARIUS · GEMINI · CAPRICORN · CANCER · SAGITTARIUS · LEO · SCORPIO · VIRGO · LIBRA

FIRE

CARDINAL · EARTH

MASCULINE · MUTABLE · AIR

FEMININE · FIXED · WATER

The Zodiac Wheel

The relationship between each Zodiac sign and the traditional astrological groupings is made clear within the Zodiac wheel. As you read through this book you will also discover references to polar, or opposite signs, and these, too, can be easily worked out by referring to the wheel.

MYTHS & LEGENDS

THE ZODIAC, WHICH IS SAID TO HAVE ORIGINATED IN
BABYLON POSSIBLY AS MANY AS 2,500 YEARS AGO, IS
A CIRCLE OF CONSTELLATIONS THROUGH WHICH THE SUN
MOVES DURING THE COURSE OF A YEAR.

The constellation of Sagittarius first seems to have been identified and named in Babylon. The symbolic centaur with his bow began to appear in Ancient Egypt much later than the time when he was carved on Babylonian boundary stones. The origin of the sign is, however, shrouded in considerable mystery, and there is no myth firmly associated with it.

Ancient Greece and Rome

In Ancient Greece, Sagittarius seems to have been a satyr: in particular, one called Crotus, who lived on Mount Helicon with his foster sisters, the Muses. The satyrs were attendants of the god Dionysus; they had goats' legs and the tails of horses, and were much given to riotous living. In those days, Sagittarius had only two legs.

Later on, Manilius, the Roman writer who in the first century B.C. set down several astrological myths, and the great astronomer Hipparchus, saw him as a four-footed centaur. The centaurs, who were also attendants of Dionysus, lived in Thessaly. Their heads and torsos were human, but the rest of their bodies were those of horses. It seems likely that the legend of the centaurs arose around a tribe of cow herders who lived in Thessaly. Indeed, the name "centaurs" can be translated as "those who round up bulls". Like the American cowboys, the Thessalonian herders rode on horseback when they were attending to their livestock.

In general, centaurs were thought to revel in cruelty, and to indulge frequently in bouts of frenzied lechery and drunkenness.

Cheiron the centaur

Some astrologers like to insist that the original Sagittarius was a centaur named Cheiron, who seems to have had nothing in common with the

Achilles and Cheiron

This late-Roman image shows Cheiron schooling Achilles in the art of riding. Cheiron was responsible for the education of both Achilles and another great hero, Jason.

ordinary centaurs except his body. Although the centaur was generally considered to be a barbarous beast, his human association made Cheiron kindly, learned, and a good friend to many gods and heroes.

Tutor of Jason and Achilles

Skilled in many arts, including that of prophesy, Cheiron taught such famous heroes as Jason, who captured the Golden Fleece, and Achilles, who was killed by a fatal arrowshot to his legendary vulnerable heel during the capture of Troy. Cheiron fed the young Achilles on a diet that consisted of the entrails of lions and the marrow bones of bears in order to give the boy

courage, and taught him the valuable arts of riding, healing, hunting, and playing the pipes.

Cheiron was an immortal but, after being accidentally injured by one of the hero Heracles's deadly poisoned arrows, he was in such profound pain, and was so afraid that his wound would never again heal, that he gave away the gift of his immortality to the suffering Prometheus, father of all the arts and sciences.

Zeus, the king of the gods, wanted so fine a creature as Cheiron to be remembered. He therefore decided to set him in the sky as a constellation, bearing the same arrow that Heracles had used to defend Prometheus.

SAGITTARIUS
SYMBOLISM

CERTAIN HERBS, SPICES, FLOWERS, TREES, GEMS, METALS, AND
ANIMALS HAVE LONG BEEN ASSOCIATED WITH PARTICULAR
ZODIAC SIGNS. SOME ASSOCIATIONS ARE SIMPLY FUN, WHILE
OTHERS CAN BE USEFUL, FOR INSTANCE IN MEDICINE.

Flowers
*Dandelions, lime-flowers, carnations,
and pinks are all flowers traditionally
associated with Sagittarius.*

DANDELION FLOWER

DANDELION SEED

CARNATIONS

Trees
Sagittarian trees include the oak, birch, lime, mulberry, chestnut, and ash.

Herbs
Lemon balm is a Sagittarian herb. A syrup made from it, with sugar added, was once kept in every house to relieve a weak stomach and general sickness.

BIRCH

OAK

Spices
No spices are particularly associated with Sagittarius, but allspice is sometimes mentioned in connection with this sign.

LEMON BALM

ALLSPICE

SAGITTARIUS
SYMBOLISM

GUN DOG
BROOCH

DEER BROOCH

INDIAN HORSE
SPICE BOX

BRONZE STAG'S HEAD

Gems

The topaz is the Sagittarian gem. To be used as a talisman, it should come from Spain, a Sagittarian country.

TOPAZ

UNREFINED TIN

Animals

All animals related to hunting, including big and small game and horses, fall under the dominion of Sagittarius.

ANCIENT GREEK BRONZE HORSES

Metal

The Sagittarian metal is traditionally said to be tin; it is especially relevant to the sign when it is highly polished and shining.

SAGITTARIUS
PROFILE

HAPPY-GO-LUCKY SAGITTARIANS GIVE THE IMPRESSION THAT
THEY HAVE NOT A CARE IN THE WORLD. THEY ARE
ALWAYS READY TO OFFER A FRIENDLY SMILE AND A WORD OF
ENCOURAGEMENT TO LESS POSITIVE PEOPLE.

Y ou are likely to possess a very firm stance, with your feet apart, and your hands on your hips. You probably hold your head high, seeming to peer towards some distant horizon.

The Sagittarian face
Wavy hair and, in men, a beard are typical of the Sagittarian face.

The body

The Sagittarian body is often somewhat thick-set, and usually very muscular. It is, perhaps, a body designed less for office work than for sport and physical activity. There have been numerous great Sagittarian dancers and basket-ball players.

Your legs are likely to be long. The Sagittarian hips and thighs are often particularly strong, but sometimes rather too prominent, much to the annoyance of many women of the sign. If you spend all of your time

following intellectual pursuits, you may develop a rather round-shouldered stoop.

The face

A number of distinctive features characterize the Sagittarian face. Your hair could be wavy and thick, and perhaps a little difficult to control. A broad, open forehead is likely to enhance your generally optimistic expression, and your eyes will probably be set wide apart, beneath straight eyebrows. Your lips are likely to be firm, and will easily break into a relaxed smile.

Style

Sagittarians often tend to cling to a "student" image, and may sport a college scarf long after they are well

16

The Sagittarian stance

A firm stance, with feet spread wide apart, hands placed on hips, and head held high, is typically Sagittarian.

established in the world. You are very likely to hate wearing formal clothes and, whenever possible, will dress as casually as you possibly can. Polo-neck sweaters are very popular among Sagittarian men and women.

Clothing that permits ease of movement is advisable for you. It is, in fact, extremely important for your clothing to be comfortable, since anything restrictive will leave you feeling intolerably claustrophobic. Perhaps your clothes will be in royal blue or purple, which are favourite Sagittarian colours.

In general

Sagittarians are not too concerned about their appearance; their outlook on life usually leads them to concentrate on other, more interesting things. Even those who are fashion-minded like to choose a number of garments at one session, so that they can then forget about clothes and get on with their lives. Similarly, you will no doubt want to be able to put on your clothes first thing in the morning, and then not have to worry

about them again until the evening. You may be perfectly happy wearing comfortable jogging clothes or track-suits most of the time, and they can sometimes be quite fashionable.

The independent Sagittarian spirit does not encourage conformity. You should therefore be careful if you decide to bend the rules when, for instance, deciding what clothes to wear for work.

SAGITTARIUS
PERSONALITY

SAGITTARIANS ARE AT THEIR BEST WHEN CHALLENGED. YOUR POSITIVE MIND WILL ALLOW YOU TO GRASP THE OVERALL STRUCTURE OF A SITUATION AND ASSESS THE BEST WAY OF SOLVING A PROBLEM, WHATEVER THE DIFFICULTIES.

People of your Sun sign sometimes seem to possess the secret of eternal youth, and may appear to be perpetual students. If you are asked what you are planning for the coming months, you will almost certainly mention some study group, class, or series of lectures that you are planning to attend. If you are not the kind of person to become involved in intellectual pursuits, you will be eager to talk about the new sports club that you have just joined.

At work

The duality of Sagittarius makes for an interesting influence, since it accentuates versatility. Many people of your Sun sign are likely to enjoy two quite separate occupations, or at least a considerable amount of variety within one.

You are often at your best expressing a number of varied talents. You may complete a task, and then turn to something that puts a very different set of demands on other skills that you might have.

Your attitudes

Sagittarians usually need to be stimulated both mentally and physically. There are, however, certain types of Sagittarian who are attracted almost exclusively to either physical or mental activities.

There are the bookish types who do not care for anything resembling physical exercise, and there are the sports fiends who enjoy participating in heavy team games, even when they are well past their prime. Both types of Sagittarian may tend to hang on to their youth.

Most Sagittarians obtain a great deal of pleasure from travelling and, if it is not possible for you to do so, you will probably turn to travel books and videos as an alternative. You may have a flair for languages, and could

Jupiter rules Sagittarius
*Jupiter, the Roman god of philosophy and languages,
represents the Sagittarian ruling planet. It can make
its subjects optimistic and loyal, but sometimes conceited.*

do far worse than to invest some of
your time and money in refining this
particular skill.

The overall picture

Sagittarian enthusiasm is usually
boundless and infectious, and it may
be expressed through risk-taking,
often of a physical nature. You must
be careful to ensure that such risks are
always extremely carefully calculated.
You could also enjoy having a small
gamble from time to time, and some
Sagittarians may even be unlucky
enough to find the idea thoroughly
irresistible. If such a tendency is not
controlled, it can cause problems for
weaker-minded Sagittarians.

SAGITTARIUS
ASPIRATIONS

YOU WILL BE HAPPIEST IN A CAREER THAT CAN BE PLANNED IN
ADVANCE. PREDICTABILITY DOES NOT OTHERWISE APPEAL,
HOWEVER, AND YOU MUST BE FREE TO DO THINGS IN YOUR OWN
WAY. IT IS EXCELLENT IF YOUR WORK INVOLVES TRAVEL.

Veterinarians
*A love for animals, especially horses
and dogs, is a powerful Sagittarian
trait. It encourages many
Sagittarians to become dedicated
veterinary surgeons.*

VETERINARY MEDICINES

Teaching
*The centaur, which symbolizes this sign,
was at one time the symbol of education.
Many Sagittarians occupy teaching posts,
often specializing in languages.*

BLACKBOARD AND CHALK

MODEL JET
LINER

The travel industry
Sagittarians enjoy travelling, and like to broaden their horizons both intellectually and physically. They therefore make excellent couriers and guides.

The law
Because most Sagittarians enjoy argument and debate, and usually have no difficulty in expressing their opinions, they make excellent advocates.

HARDBACK
BOOKS

Publishing
To expand their own knowledge, and to encourage others to do the same, is a powerful Sagittarian motivation. Many people of this Sun sign are therefore attracted to publishing.

LEGAL
DOCUMENTS

SAGITTARIUS
HEALTH

YOUR DUAL SAGITTARIAN NATURE INCLINES YOU TO BE SPORTY
AND PHYSICALLY ACTIVE, AS WELL AS STUDIOUS AND
INTELLECTUAL. IDEALLY, YOU SHOULD AIM TO KEEP THESE
CHARACTERISTICS IN BALANCE.

Sagittarians need to exploit their physical and intellectual energy. They have excellent resources of both, and it is a great pity if they are not fully developed. Because your outlook is generally positive and enthusiastic, you respond well when you are challenged.

Your diet
The Sagittarian body area is traditionally said to cover the hips and thighs and, because a fairly rich, somewhat heavy diet is preferred by people of this sign, weight gain can sometimes be a problem for them.

You are likely to benefit from the cell salt Kali Muriaticum (Kali Mur.), which may help prevent bronchial congestion and swollen glands.

Taking care
The Sagittarian body organ is the liver. You should make a special effort to learn what does and does not agree with you, and find out exactly what your food and drink limits are. It could also be a good idea for you to always have supply of hangover remedies in the bathroom cupboard; you might even develop one of your own. Restlessness can be a problem for Sagittarians. You may find it hard to really relax; a complete change of occupation usually works well in these cases.

Asparagus
Sagittarian foods include onions, asparagus, and tomatoes.

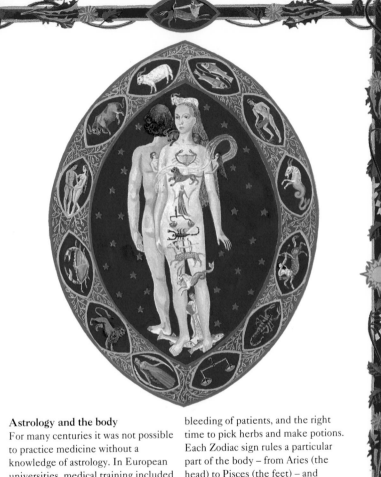

Astrology and the body

For many centuries it was not possible to practice medicine without a knowledge of astrology. In European universities, medical training included information on how planetary positions would affect the administration of medicines, the bleeding of patients, and the right time to pick herbs and make potions. Each Zodiac sign rules a particular part of the body – from Aries (the head) to Pisces (the feet) – and textbooks always included a drawing of a "Zodiac man" (or woman) that illustrated the point.

SAGITTARIUS AT
LEISURE

EACH OF THE SUN SIGNS TRADITIONALLY SUGGESTS SPARE-TIME
ACTIVITIES, HOBBIES, AND HOLIDAY DESTINATIONS.
ALTHOUGH THESE ARE ONLY SUGGESTIONS, THEY OFTEN WORK
OUT WELL, AND ARE WORTH TESTING.

Travel
*Hungary, Australia, and Spain are
among the countries ruled by
Sagittarius. Spain is a top favourite
for Sagittarian holidays.*

POSTAGE STAMPS

Reading
*Sagittarians are eternal
students, who love to
study – especially foreign
languages. You will
therefore enjoy reading.*

BOOKS

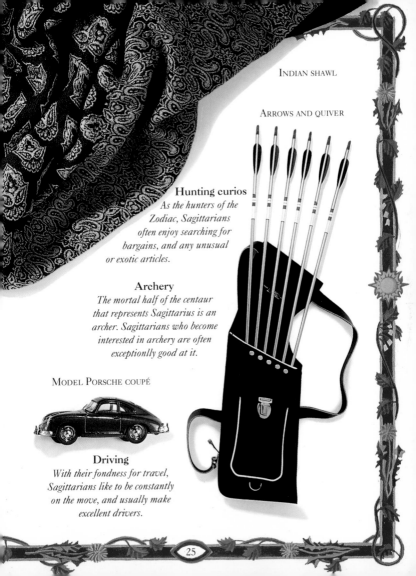

ARROWS AND QUIVER

Hunting curios

As the hunters of the Zodiac, Sagittarians often enjoy searching for bargains, and any unusual or exotic articles.

Archery

The mortal half of the centaur that represents Sagittarius is an archer. Sagittarians who become interested in archery are often exceptionlly good at it.

MODEL PORSCHE COUPÉ

Driving

With their fondness for travel, Sagittarians like to be constantly on the move, and usually make excellent drivers.

25

SAGITTARIUS IN
LOVE

TRADITIONALLY, SAGITTARIANS ARE THE HUNTERS OF THE
ZODIAC. IN LOVE, AS IN OTHER AREAS OF THEIR LIVES,
THE CHALLENGE OF THE CHASE IS ALL-ENGROSSING, AND
MAY EVEN BE MORE EXCITING THAN THE CAPTURE.

The Sagittarian love of challenge can be ignited if the object of your affection plays hard to get. This may be very exciting for you.

As a lover
A Sagittarian's natural enthusiasm for love and sex is very infectious, and it is not difficult for people of your Sun sign to attract partners. Your need for your own space, and for a relationship without even a hint of claustrophobia, is very important. You really cannot bear to feel restricted, and your partners must realize this and allow you a measure of independence if the relationship is to last.

Once they have tamed their coltish attitudes, Sagittarians make very rewarding partners because of their love of life, optimism, and ability to encourage partners to pursue their own interests.

Types of Sagittarian lover
The influence of other planets encourages every Zodiac type to express love in one of five different ways, and it is usually fairly easy to recognize the group to which you belong. Some Sagittarians are really romantic, and go for affairs with all the memorable trimmings. They either rush into

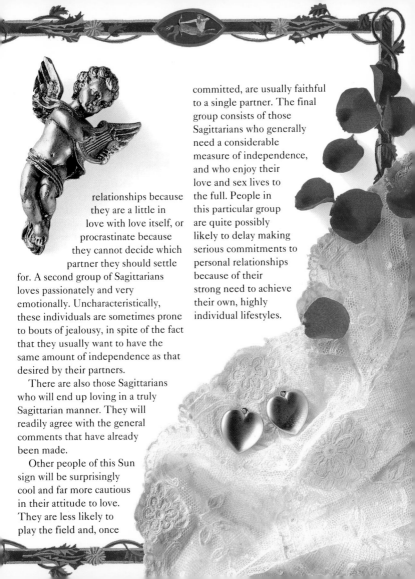

committed, are usually faithful to a single partner. The final group consists of those Sagittarians who generally need a considerable measure of independence, and who enjoy their love and sex lives to the full. People in this particular group are quite possibly likely to delay making serious commitments to personal relationships because of their strong need to achieve their own, highly individual lifestyles.

relationships because they are a little in love with love itself, or procrastinate because they cannot decide which partner they should settle for. A second group of Sagittarians loves passionately and very emotionally. Uncharacteristically, these individuals are sometimes prone to bouts of jealousy, in spite of the fact that they usually want to have the same amount of independence as that desired by their partners.

There are also those Sagittarians who will end up loving in a truly Sagittarian manner. They will readily agree with the general comments that have already been made.

Other people of this Sun sign will be surprisingly cool and far more cautious in their attitude to love. They are less likely to play the field and, once

SAGITTARIUS AT
HOME

ANY SAGITTARIAN HOME WILL FEEL VERY ROOMY, PERHAPS
BECAUSE OF A CLEVER USE OF MIRRORS. THIS IS JUST
AS WELL, BECAUSE FURNITURE, BOOKS, ORNAMENTS, AND
CHINA WILL OCCUPY EVERY SPARE CORNER.

The Sagittarian home is usually marked by a definite tendency to steer clear of anything that might result in a rather claustrophobic atmosphere. Large windows, and spacious, open-plan living are therefore given substantial priority.

Globe of the world
A love of travel is often reflected in the Sagittarian choice of objects or pictures.

Furniture
You are one of the hunters of the Zodiac, and probably love to visit street markets and antique shops in search of bargains that suit your taste and practical needs. Sagittarians usually choose furniture that is not particularly adventurous, but that is built to last. While you like to be reasonably comfortable, space for bookshelves, or simply piles of books,

and places to keep the articles of sports equipment that are so much a part of the Sagittarian lifestyle, are just as, or perhaps even more, important.

Soft furnishings
The cushions in your home may appear somewhat crumpled and well used, but they will invite people to sit down. Many items, such as oriental rugs, will have originated overseas, and the fabric for the curtains will sometimes have a rather unusual design. Sagittarians often favour the strong, energetic, perennial designs of William Morris, which reflect Sagittarian energy and a liking for warm colour. Dark blue and purple are popular, and those of this

sign usually like the yellows, reds, and golds of the fire element that influences their personalities.

Decorative objects

Because most Sagittarians have lively minds, the decorative items that enhance your home, and certainly the overall effect, will often arouse interest and intellectual discussion among those who come to visit. The pictures that you choose are often open landscapes, since Sagittarians cannot bear anything claustrophobic.

There will almost certainly be interesting, rather than purely beautiful, travel souvenirs. Many Sagittarians enjoy playing the guitar, and one may therefore be given pride

of place in your home. Either books or sporting trophies, or perhaps even both, may be present, depending on whether you are a bookish or an athletic type of Sagittarian. There may also be a fair variety of objects scattered around your home that represent your own religious faith, such as crucifixes or icons.

Tidiness is not a characteristic that one would immediately associate with a Sagittarian home; you are very likely to place the objects in it indiscriminately, and then to continually shuffle them around.

Guitar, rug, and chest
Sagittarians may give a guitar pride of place; a Spanish influence may also be evident.

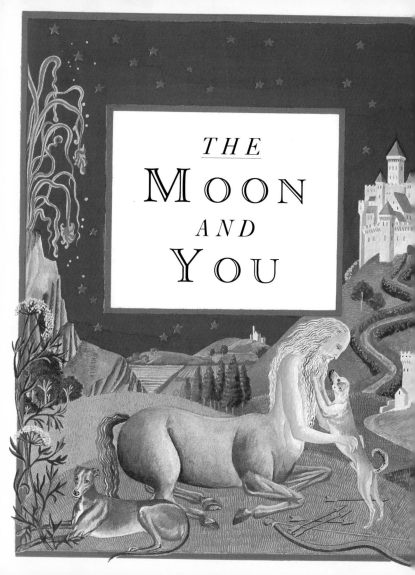

THE
MOON
AND
YOU

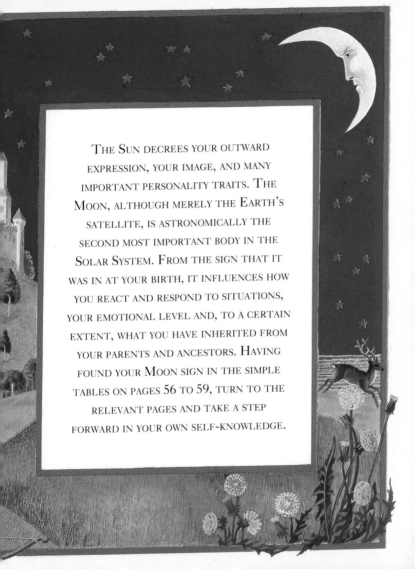

THE SUN DECREES YOUR OUTWARD
EXPRESSION, YOUR IMAGE, AND MANY
IMPORTANT PERSONALITY TRAITS. THE
MOON, ALTHOUGH MERELY THE EARTH'S
SATELLITE, IS ASTRONOMICALLY THE
SECOND MOST IMPORTANT BODY IN THE
SOLAR SYSTEM. FROM THE SIGN THAT IT
WAS IN AT YOUR BIRTH, IT INFLUENCES HOW
YOU REACT AND RESPOND TO SITUATIONS,
YOUR EMOTIONAL LEVEL AND, TO A CERTAIN
EXTENT, WHAT YOU HAVE INHERITED FROM
YOUR PARENTS AND ANCESTORS. HAVING
FOUND YOUR MOON SIGN IN THE SIMPLE
TABLES ON PAGES 56 TO 59, TURN TO THE
RELEVANT PAGES AND TAKE A STEP
FORWARD IN YOUR OWN SELF-KNOWLEDGE.

THE MOON IN
ARIES

BOTH THE SUN AND THE MOON WERE IN FIRE SIGNS AT THE
TIME OF YOUR BIRTH. IT IS THEREFORE LIKELY THAT YOU
HAVE AN ENTHUSIASTIC AND OPTIMISTIC OUTLOOK ON LIFE,
AND IMMEDIATE REACTIONS TO SITUATIONS.

Some aspects of your character may have been tempered by a number of strong influences in your birth chart. Otherwise you are likely to be a lively and extrovert person.

Self-expression
You are always ready to accept daunting challenges at a moment's notice. In fact, you often throw yourself in at the deep end, without thinking about the consequences.

Perhaps even more than most Sagittarians, you have breadth of vision and the ability to grasp the essentials of a situation. But having done so, the details may defeat you; therefore either make sure that you leave them to someone else, or discipline yourself to cope with them.

Romance
Your fiery enthusiasm for love and sex should ensure that you obtain a lot of pleasure out of this sphere of your

life. You may not always take your relationships too seriously, since your passion has a lighthearted air.

Be aware that the worst Arien fault is selfishness, and that you may sometimes react to your lovers in a somewhat selfish way. You certainly need a partner who can match your abundant Sagittarian and Arien emotional and physical energy, and sheer enjoyment of love and sex.

Your well-being
The Arien body area is the head, and you could be rather prone to headaches. Perhaps these are due to your frustration at other people's incompetence or their slowness to respond to you. Alternatively, you may suffer from a slight kidney upset and, if your headaches persist, you should get a medical check-up.

Anyone with an Arien influence may, because of a tendency to be too hasty, be somewhat accident-prone.

The Moon in Aries

Minor cuts and burns, and knocks when driving, can easily occur. An awareness of this tendency will help you to combat it. You are pretty energetic, physically, and should have a fairly fast metabolism.

Planning ahead

Sagittarians love a gamble, and with an Arien Moon this tendency is exacerbated. While you could well enjoy investment, your enterprising spirit may be marred by this gambling streak. Therefore resist seductive schemes that may well be far less rewarding than they sound, and take professional advice in this sphere.

Parenthood

You make an excellent parent, and will be as young at heart as your children, encouraging them greatly in all their interests. You should have few generation gap problems. In fact, the reverse may be true; you might have to remind yourself of your age.

THE MOON IN
TAURUS

YOUR TAUREAN MOON STABILIZES YOUR FIERY CHARACTERISTICS,
ESPECIALLY WHEN YOU ARE CONFRONTED BY CHALLENGES.
IT ALSO HELPS TO CURB UNNECCESSARY RISK-TAKING AND A
TENDENCY TO BE BLINDLY OPTIMISTIC.

The Moon is, according to traditional astrology, "well placed" in Taurus. As a result, its influence on you is rather stronger than it is on other Sagittarians.

Self-expression

Like Sagittarius, Taurus is an earth sign. It prevents you from taking premature action, and instills caution, common sense, and even a good measure of patience – not a quality that one naturally associates with Sun sign Sagittarians. Your response to most situations is not to get immediately involved. You will give yourself time to assess a situation before allowing your natural verve and enthusiasm, springing from your Sagittarian Sun sign, to emerge.

Romance

You have the warm affection usually associated with Taurus, and it is this that will first emerge when you develop an emotional relationship. Your Taurean Moon adds a great deal of natural charm to your personality, while removing nothing of the sexiness of your Sagittarian Sun.

Bear in mind that the worst Taurean fault is possessiveness. As a Sagittarian with an instinctive love of freedom, you detest this unacceptable trait, but your Moon can edge you towards it. Recognize the fact, and watch for the signs.

Your well-being

The Taurean body area is the throat, and you probably find that colds start there. You may also have trouble with your tonsils.

Those with a Taurean emphasis tend to put on weight easily, often because they have a sweet tooth. Sagittarians like rich, hearty food, so you may need to keep a constant calorie check if you want to retain your good figure. Do not let the

The Moon in Taurus

relaxed attitude of your Taurean Moon get the better of you where exercise is concerned. Sagittarians must never stagnate.

Planning ahead

You are cautious and have good business sense. As a result you can cope with money far better than many Sun sign Sagittarians. Even if you do succumb to your Sagittarian gambling instinct, the chances are that you will not fritter away more money than you can afford to lose.

Parenthood

As a parent, you no doubt get things just about right, and will discipline your children in precisely the right way, so that they know exactly where they stand with you.

The power of your Sagittarian Sun makes you an optimistic and very encouraging parent, and your children thrive on your constructive comments and warm affection. You do not find it difficult to keep up with their ideas, and are unlikely to incur problems with the generation gap.

THE MOON IN
GEMINI

SAGITTARIUS AND GEMINI ARE POLAR OR OPPOSITE ZODIAC SIGNS,
SO YOU WERE BORN UNDER A FULL MOON. RESTLESSNESS IS A
GEMINIAN CHARACTERISTIC, AND YOU SHOULD TRY TO FIGHT IT.
BE VERSATILE, BUT DEVELOP CONSISTENCY OF EFFORT.

Each of us is, in one way or another, liable to express the attributes of our polar, or opposite, Zodiac sign. Each sign has its partner across the horoscope; for Sagittarians, this is Gemini and, because the Moon was in Gemini when you were born, this polarity is emphasized in an interesting and powerful way.

Self-expression

Sagittarius and Gemini are both mutable signs, which means that you are flexible and intellectual in character, and have a versatile mind. These signs are also traditionally dual in nature, and you may therefore have a tendency to do more than one thing at a time. This is probably very natural to you, and it is something that you should not try to curb. You must, however, work to avoid superficiality, which may also result from your dual nature. Always make a special effort to complete everything

that you undertake. Also remember that restlessness is the worst fault of both Gemini and Sagittarius. This characteristic is further emphasized in people born under a Full Moon.

Romance

You have all the passion of your Sagittarian Sun to express in your love and sex life, added to which your Geminian Moon will make you very flirtatious. Some duality can obviously find a place in this area of your life, and it is worth remembering that you could encounter problems if you do not keep these tendencies under control. Even more than most Sagittarians, you require a good level of intellectual rapport with a lover.

Your well-being

Gemini rules the arms and hands, so yours may be vulnerable to injury. It also rules the lungs, so you could be susceptible to bronchitis, and should

The Moon in Gemini

beware of a cough that will not go away. If you smoke, cut down on the habit as soon as possible.

Your Geminian Moon gives you a great deal of nervous energy, which must be positively expressed through lively physical exercise.

Planning ahead

You should probably always seek professional advice when you have money to invest. Your Sagittarian gambling spirit may combine with a Geminian liking for get-rich-quick schemes and, as a result, you could end up losing far more money than you are really able to afford.

Parenthood

As a parent, you may even be ahead of your children in relation to the most modern trends.

It is, however, possible that a tendency to be inconsistent may damage your relationship. Make sure that your children always know where they stand with you. In this way you should avoid the generation gap.

THE MOON IN
CANCER

YOU REALLY NEED INDEPENDENCE, FREEDOM OF EXPRESSION,
AND EMOTIONAL SECURITY. YOUR URGE FOR THESE IS
INSTINCTIVE AND POWERFUL. YOU ARE PROTECTIVE TOWARDS
THOSE YOU LOVE, AND VALUE SOLIDARITY.

The combination of Sagittarius, a fire sign, and Cancer, a water sign, makes for some contrasting characteristics that you should use to full advantage. Because the Moon rules Cancer, the influence of your Moon sign is very powerful.

Self-expression
You are much more sensitive than many Sagittarians, and can be more easily hurt, too. You are also prone to changes of mood. While you will have plenty of Sagittarian optimism and enthusiasm, your immediate reaction to any situation will be cautious. You have an instinctive self-defensive system that immediately springs into action when you are challenged.

Romance
You express love very sensually, and have many desirable qualities that should enable you to maintain a stable, yet exciting, relationship.

Your emotional level is very high, for you have all the powerful, fiery emotion of Sagittarius, which will spur you into passionate expression of love and sex. You also have the more tender emotion of Cancer, which should enable you to tune into your partner's needs on all levels.

You are probably less happy-go-lucky in your relationships than many Sun sign Sagittarians, but should be careful not to let Cancerian moodiness and a tendency to react very sharply mar so much that is positive.

Your well-being
The Cancerian body area covers the breasts and, although Cancerians are no more likely to contract cancer than anyone else, women Sagittarians should obviously make the usual regular checks.

Sagittarians are among the people who are least likely to worry when confronted with problems, whereas

The Moon in Cancer

Cancerians are among those most prone to it. The positive areas of your personality should enable you to deal with worry, although your digestion may sometimes trouble you under difficult circumstances.

Cancerians are usually good and enthusiastic cooks, and Sagittarians like tasty, rich food. If you are overweight, you may not be taking enough exercise.

Planning ahead

You are very lucky where finance is concerned. Your Sagittarian gambling spirit is mitigated by a shrewd and instinctive business sense, stemming from your Moon sign. If you are investing, follow your intuition; when you are in doubt, you would be wise to seek professional advice.

Parenthood

You are probably a rather more caring and protective parent than most Sagittarians. Try not to take this too far, though, and let your enthusiasm encourage your children. If you are not too sentimental, and manage to keep abreast of your children's thoughts and ideas, you will have few problems with the generation gap.

THE MOON IN
LEO

YOUR LEO MOON PROMPTS A WELL-ORGANIZED, RATHER FORMAL
APPROACH TO MOST SITUATIONS. YOUR ACCEPTANCE OF
CHALLENGE IS ENCOURAGED BY AN ABILITY TO TAKE COMMAND,
BUT YOU MUST TAKE CARE TO AVOID BEING BOSSY.

Your Sun and Moon signs are both of the fire element, so you have great natural enthusiasm and optimism, and an extremely positive outlook on life.

Self-expression
You may tend to be marginally more conventional than most Sun sign Sagittarians, but this only serves to make you naturally elegant, and gives you a powerful instinct for real quality. Your Sun sign, on the other hand, endows you with a good mind, and you may have very considerable creative potential.

You are able to cope well with people, and very possibly have excellent organizational ability. Generally speaking, your Sagittarian Sun prevents you from becoming pompous or bossy, but should you be accused of these traits, take note. You are extremely magnanimous, and never harbour a grudge.

Romance
You are a very passionate and demonstrative lover, and probably have a stylish approach to a prospective partner. You will create an expensive, romantic atmosphere, and will do everything in your power to make life happy, enjoyable, and even blissful for your lovers.

You will be a very supportive partner, and because loyalty is important to you, once you are committed you have less of a roving eye than many Sagittarians.

Your well-being
The Leo body area covers the back and spine. You will do well to remember this, and to gear part of your exercise schedule towards that area. If you have to spend a lot of time sitting at an office desk, consider getting a backrest chair. The Leo organ is the heart, and it too must be kept in good condition.

The Moon in Leo

Most Sun sign Sagittarians not only need, but also enjoy, physical exercise. Keeping fit through sports and exercise should therefore be no real problem for you. Your Leo Moon may attract you to all kinds of dance, and this is something that you should consider as an alternative to health clubs or participating in team games.

Planning ahead

You need to earn a lot of money in order to enjoy a comfortable lifestyle; you have big ideas, and may well be very extravagant. But you are not without financial flair, and can be clever with investments, provided that you remember to control your Sagittarian gambling spirit, and the tendency to put too many eggs in one basket. Aim to have one or two really sound, secure savings schemes.

Parenthood

You are a very encouraging and enthusiastic parent, and your children will thrive on your positive, lively comments on their interests. At times your children may see you as slightly pompous, but if you keep a sense of humour you should not have many problems with the generation gap.

THE MOON IN
VIRGO

Do not hesitate when confronted by tricky situations —
you may have a tendency to underestimate yourself.
Guard against tension and restlessness. You are a good
communicator, and can cope well with detail.

Both Sagittarius and Virgo are mutable signs and, as a result, you have a flexible mind and great intellectual capacity.

Self-expression

While most Sagittarians find detail boring and difficult to deal with, you respond differently. You react well to it, and may look at details even before looking for a broad overview.

You are critical and analytical in your approach to problems, and will probably express your Sagittarian versatility within the broad confines of one or two large subjects. Your ability to get your ideas across to other people is excellent, since you communicate fluently.

Romance

Your Sagittarian passion is somewhat moderated by your Virgoan Moon, which may inhibit you in the area of love and sex. An instinctive modesty

can make you feel a little inferior in this field. In fact, you have much to offer, so try not to put yourself down.

A serious Virgoan fault is to carp at and to criticize partners, often for no good reason. Your Sagittarian Sun sign will loathe this tendency, and help you to bite your tongue if you find yourself beginning to nag.

Your well-being

The Virgoan body area is the stomach and, while Sagittarius is not prone to worry, Virgo certainly is. Interestingly, your stomach may react before your mind. You need a high-fibre diet, and perhaps incline to vegetarianism, since Virgoans are particularly attracted to this.

You have a great deal of nervous, tense energy, and periods of stress can wreak havoc with you. A calming, centring discipline such as yoga could well be of considerable benefit to you. Also think about sports and exercise

The Moon in Virgo

regimens, which could include pursuits such as walking, rambling, cycling, and gardening.

Planning ahead

You are more careful with your finances than most Sagittarians, and find it fairly easy to save money and to avoid unnecessary extravagance. Your ability to cope with detail may incline you to keep careful accounts, and to watch the stock market. Do, however, guard against your Sagittarian gambling spirit, and be self-critical if it seems likely to run away with you. This will be the time to take professional advice.

Parenthood

All your Sagittarian enthusiasm will colour your attitude to your children. However, that Virgoan critical response may be far harsher in your children's eyes than it seems to you. Keep up with their concerns, and you will avoid the generation gap.

THE MOON IN
LIBRA

YOUR REACTION TO ALMOST ANY SITUATION IS LIKELY TO BE VERY
LAID BACK. ALWAYS MAKE SURE THAT YOU EXPRESS
YOUR SPLENDID SAGITTARIAN POTENTIAL, AND NEVER ALLOW
YOUR MIND AND BODY TO STAGNATE.

The fire of your Sagittarian Sun and the air of your Libran Moon blend well. You have a warm-hearted and attractive personality, and respond well to people, showing sympathy and understanding.

Self-expression

Because of their characteristic haste, Sagittarians sometimes tend to lack tact. This is not so in your case; your Libran Moon helps you to control the tendency and, in many ways, makes you a diplomat.

When confronted with challenging situations, your immediate response may well be less assertive and positive than that of many Sun sign Sagittarians. However, once you have drawn your conclusions, your Sagittarian Sun sign usually points you in the right direction.

There is an easygoing side to your nature, and you could give the impression that you cannot be rushed.

You may need to persuade yourself to be a little more self-disciplined and better organized if you are to get the best out of your potential.

Romance

You are probably rather more romantic than many Sagittarians, and enjoy setting a glamorous scene in which to make love. Once committed, you make a wonderful partner. You will always be fair and listen to your lover's ideas.

Your well-being

The Libran organ is the kidneys and, if you are at all prone to headaches, there could be a minor problem with them. Very often those with a Libran influence get terribly bored with exercise, and just give up. Aim to avoid this, because Sagittarians have a lot of physical energy to burn, and lethargy does not suit them. Your Libran Moon may encourage you to

The Moon in Libra

eat too much sweet food, and you could well suffer from excessive weight gain as a result. Redress the balance by becoming a member of a good health club with a variety of exercise programmes.

Planning ahead

You are very generous and may not be terribly sensible with money. Both your Sagittarian gambling streak, and your Libran Moon's sympathy for a hard-luck story, may be a source of money problems. Do not over-invest in one area, do not lend money, and do not gamble more than you can afford to lose. Always aim to get professional advice in this area.

Parenthood

While you are a very enthusiastic and kind parent, you are capable of spoiling your children. Remember that indecisiveness on your part makes it difficult for them to know where they stand. If you keep up with their ideas, you will have few difficulties with the generation gap.

THE MOON IN
SCORPIO

YOUR SAGITTARIAN BREADTH OF VISION IS ENHANCED BY A NATURAL
ABILITY TO DELVE DEEPLY INTO PROBLEMS. THIS DERIVES
FROM YOUR MOON SIGN. YOU HAVE AN INTENSE, FIERY PASSION,
BUT YOU SHOULD CURB ANY TENDENCY TO JEALOUSY.

Sagittarius and Scorpio are both charged with a great deal of physical and emotional energy. Sagittarians express this in a lively, positive way, while Scorpios tend to be deeply penetrating, incisive, and generally very intuitive.

Self-expression

You obviously have extremely powerful resources on which to draw, and striking potential. You have breadth of vision, and the ability to deal with any aspect of a challenge or problematic situation. Your powers of endurance, under both difficult physical conditions, and intellectually demanding ones, are second to none. With all of this in mind, it is obvious that you need to be totally committed to your objectives in life, and that your reach must always exceed your grasp. If you are unfulfilled, and life seems empty, few Sagittarians will suffer more than you.

Romance

Your passion for a full life is second only to your expression of love and sex. In this area you are very much a whole-hogger and, while you contribute much towards the success of a permanent emotional relationship, you are also very demanding, and need an extremely energetic and passionate partner.

The worst Scorpio fault is jealousy – something that your Sagittarian Sun sign will deplore. You may find yourself reacting negatively to a partner's mildly flirtatious behaviour, while you yourself enjoy an element of freedom within a relationship.

Your well-being

The Scorpio body area covers the genitals; anyone, whatever their Sun sign, should get regular checks in that area. But it is your emotional and physical energy that has the strongest influence on your general health and

The Moon in Scorpio

well-being. Aim to take regular
exercise; all kinds of water sports
should suit you.

Planning ahead

You could be very clever with money,
provided that you allow your
instinctive business sense and
intuition to express themselves.
Financial risk-taking could attract
you, and you may end up taking an
unwise plunge. At such times, the
Scorpion is wiser than the Centaur.

Parenthood

While you are always enthusiastic and
encouraging, you could be a
somewhat demanding parent.
Children like a well-structured life,
which gives them a sense of security.
Be careful not to overdo this,
however, or to allow tradition and
discipline to interfere with the sheer
enjoyment of your children's
company. Encourage their interests
and ideas, and keep abreast of them
in order to avoid the generation gap.

THE MOON IN
SAGITTARIUS

BECAUSE BOTH THE SUN AND THE MOON WERE IN SAGITTARIUS
AT THE TIME OF YOUR BIRTH, YOU WERE BORN UNDER A
NEW MOON. SAGITTARIUS IS A FIRE SIGN, SO THIS ELEMENT
INFLUENCES YOUR PERSONALITY AND REACTIONS.

Should you study a list of your Sun sign characteristics, you will probably recognize that a great many of them apply to you. Out of a list of perhaps 20 traits of a Sun sign listed in books or magazines, most people will strongly identify with 11 or 12. For you, however, the average increases considerably because the Sun and Moon were both in Sagittarius when you were born.

Self-expression
Not only do you have the attributes of your Sun sign, but you also respond to situations in the same manner. When someone puts an idea to you, your natural enthusiasm ignites, and you are keen to get involved.

 You probably do not worry too much about possible pitfalls or problems, regarding them as something to be dealt with when you come to them. But it is important that you keep your initial enthusiasm on the boil, because if you do not, you could easily succumb to the most serious Sagittarian fault: restlessness. You are capable of enormous versatility, but must learn to be selective, and to develop a degree of consistency. You have a high level of intellectual and physical energy, and neither must be allowed to stagnate.

Romance
You are passionate and will enjoy love and sex with a youthful exuberance. You must have a full love and sex life, and need a partner who is intellectually very stimulating.

 Fidelity may not come naturally to you, and your partners must learn that you need a good measure of freedom in this sphere of your life.

Your well-being
If you turn to pages 22 to 23, you will read about Sagittarian health and well-being. As you are a "double

The Moon in Sagittarius

Sagittarian", those comments will most definitely apply to you. Be careful not to over-indulge in heavy food. You are prone to weight gain, and unwanted flesh is likely to gather around your hips and thighs – especially if you are a woman. Good workouts and some of the more daring sports are excellent for you.

Planning ahead

Your Sagittarian gambling instinct could get the better of you from time to time, and you may be strongly attracted to get-rich-quick schemes. You must be careful to curb these tricky enthusiasms, and to always take professional financial advice when you have some money to invest, no matter how convincing a deal may seem at the time.

Parenthood

You are among the most enthusiastic of parents, and will always encourage your children to make the most of their potential. You probably try to see to it that they fill their days as completely as you do. You do not find it difficult to keep up with their ideas, and should not incur problems with the generation gap.

THE MOON IN
CAPRICORN

YOU HAVE A GREAT DEAL OF POTENTIAL, AND ARE ALWAYS VERY
KEEN TO GET INVOLVED IN AMBITIOUS SCHEMES. YOUR
EARTHY CAPRICORNIAN MOON ADDS PRACTICALITY TO YOUR
CHARACTER — AND PERHAPS A TENDENCY TO GRUMBLE.

There are some striking contrasts between Sagittarius and Capricorn and, as a result, you possess a multi-faceted personality, with a great deal of potential that can be expressed in a variety of ways.

Self-expression

Your Sagittarian Sun sign gives you fiery enthusiasm and a positive outlook on life. On the other hand, the earth element of your Moon sign makes you instinctively cautious, and much less likely to take risks than many Sagittarians.

You are very ambitious and, when presented with a challenging situation, will at once be able to foresee the end result. You will then begin to plan your moves towards the attainment of that goal.

Sagittarians are, on the whole, good communicators, and you will certainly let it be known if you are being impeded by some form of inefficiency. Should you be accused of grumbling too much, which is usually very uncharacteristic of Sagittarians, you should take note.

Romance

You are less gushing in expressing your emotions than many people of your Sun sign, and could tend to hold back a little in the initial stages of a relationship. This does not mean that you cannot enjoy a truly rewarding and fulfilling love and sex life.

You could be more faithful, and have less of a roving eye, than other Sagittarians, and may take a while to commit yourself to a relationship.

Your well-being

The Capricornian body area covers the knees and shins. Yours will be vulnerable, especially if you engage in a lot of sporting activities. Treatment can save a great deal of pain and the development of serious problems.

The Moon in Capricorn

The teeth, skin, and bones are also in Capricorn's domain, so beware of stiffness in the joints, and keep moving. Do not neglect regular dental check-ups, and wear a protective cream when the sun is strong.

You may have a rapid metabolism; if so, weight gain is unlikely to be a problem for you.

Planning ahead

Anyone with a Capricornian influence is usually careful, and often clever, with money. You like to see it grow, so your Sagittarian gambling streak is probably kept under control. You only take financial risks if you are sure you can afford to lose the money involved.

Parenthood

Your sense of humour is a great asset to you as a parent, but you could, surprisingly for a Sagittarian, react a little coolly to some of your children's suggestions and ideas. If you enjoy the challenge of keeping up with them, you will manage to leap across the generation gap.

THE MOON IN
AQUARIUS

SAGITTARIUS AND AQUARIUS ARE BOTH SIGNS THAT REQUIRE
INDEPENDENCE. TRY NOT TO ALLOW A TENDENCY TO
RESPOND COOLLY AND DISTANTLY TO OTHER PEOPLE TO SPOIL
YOUR WONDERFUL SAGITTARIAN APPROACH TO LOVE.

The fire element of Sagittarius and the air element of Aquarius blend well, not only making you the individualist of your Sun sign peers, but also putting you among those who greatly need independence and freedom of expression.

Self-expression

You may well have built a lifestyle that has certain individual features. You are a warm-hearted and very friendly person, but definitely need both physical and psychological space. Pettiness, unnecessary detail, and people who nag are not for you.

Romance

The Moon in Aquarius adds a certain glitz and glamour to your personality, but you may also respond coolly and distantly when first approached by prospective partners. You need a good period of friendship and intellectual rapport before the lively passion of

your Sagittarian Sun can be fully expressed. Your love and sex life are probably rewarding, but you must cater to your need for independence. You may postpone a full commitment until you find a partner who sees this, and is willing to allow you space.

Your well-being

The Aquarian body area covers the ankles, and yours are vulnerable. The circulation is also ruled by Aquarius and, if you like crisp, cold weather, you must try to keep warm.

You may enjoy skiing, skating, or dancing. In any case, you should get involved in some form of exercise. You thrive on a light diet, even if you like the heavier foods often favoured by your Sun sign.

Planning ahead

You may find it quite difficult to save money regularly. You are probably attracted to fashionable clothes and

The Moon in Aquarius

fine and unusual things for the home. You could go all out for some apparently excellent savings scheme and invest heavily in it, only to find that it runs into difficulty.

It may be well worth your while to seek professional financial advice when you have some money to invest. Best of all, you should seriously consider taking part in some scheme where a certain proportion of your regular pay-cheque is invested at the source, before you squander it.

Remember, your Sagittarian gambling spirit is very much attracted to exciting but risky schemes.

Parenthood

You are an extremely lively parent, and do not find it difficult to know what your children are thinking. If you keep up with their ideas, you should have few problems with the generation gap. Be affectionate towards your children, and avoid acting unpredictably.

THE MOON IN
PISCES

SAGITTARIUS AND PISCES ARE DUAL SIGNS OF THE ZODIAC, AND YOU
ARE THEREFORE VERY VERSATILE. HOWEVER, YOU DO NEED
TO DEVELOP CONSISTENCY OF EFFORT, AND MUST BE DISCIPLINED
IF YOU ARE TO DEVELOP TO YOUR FULL POTENTIAL.

Sagittarius and Pisces are both mutable signs, and their combination makes you very flexible and easygoing. In addition, both are dual signs. Pisces is represented by two fishes swimming in opposite directions, Sagittarius by a creature who is both man and horse. These symbols represent a high degree of versatility, with enviable potential, but suggest a similarly high degree of restlessness.

Self-expression
While it is very important for you to have a variety of very different interests, you should also develop staying power, and complete any project that you start, if it is to give you inner satisfaction.

Your response to challenges is complex. At first, you probably feel somewhat hesitant and lacking in confidence, but then you may decide on a line of action. Finally you will,

for no apparent reason, do precisely the opposite, which may turn out to be a mistake. Your Sun sign gives you an excellent, sharp intellect and a rich imagination, possibly adding creative potential. Be firm with yourself, and exploit these qualities.

Romance
You are caring, loving, and passionate, but need a strong partner who will bring out the best in you and ignite your Sagittarian enthusiasm. You are capable of giving much to a lover, and should enjoy a rich and rewarding love and sex life.

The worst Piscean fault is deceitfulness; do not lie to yourself, especially when considering your lovers' attitudes to you.

Your well-being
The Piscean body area is the feet, and you may find it difficult to obtain comfortable shoes. You could easily

The Moon in Pisces

fall back on eating too heavily, and may be prone to putting on weight unless you are actively involved in some form of sport, for example dancing or skating.

Planning ahead

You are sometimes left wondering where your money has gone. The answer is that you have spent it on frivolous things. You may need help from a stronger, more down-to-earth partner or a friendly bank manager in working out a sensible budget. If you have some spare money, make sure that you take financial advice before investing it. You should neither lend money, nor give so readily to charity that you get yourself into trouble.

Parenthood

You are probably a very warm and caring parent, who may well spoil your children. Take disciplinary measures when you must, even if you do not enjoy being strict, since this will help give your children a more secure background. You will always listen to your children's problems, so they will know where they stand with you. There should be no problems with the generation gap.

Moon Charts

THE FOLLOWING TABLES WILL ENABLE YOU TO DISCOVER YOUR
MOON SIGN. THEN, BY REFERRING TO THE PRECEDING
PAGES, YOU WILL BE ABLE TO INVESTIGATE ITS QUALITIES, AND
SEE HOW THEY WORK WITH YOUR SUN SIGN.

By referring to the Moon charts opposite and overleaf, look up the year of your birth and the Zodiacal glyph for your birth month. Refer next to the Moon Table (*below, left*) in which the days of the month are listed against a number. The number against the day of the month in which you were born indicates how many Zodiacal glyphs (*below, right*) must be counted before you reach your Moon sign. You may have to count to Pisces and return to Aries. For example, given the birthdate 21 May 1991, you initially need to find the Moon sign for the first day of May in that year. It is Sagittarius (♐). With the birthdate falling on the 21st, nine signs must be added. The Moon sign for this birth date is therefore Virgo (♍).

Moon Table

DAYS OF THE MONTH AND NUMBER OF
SIGNS THAT SHOULD BE ADDED

DAY	ADD	DAY	ADD	DAY	ADD	DAY	ADD
1	0	9	4	17	7	25	11
2	1	10	4	18	8	26	11
3	1	11	5	19	8	27	12
4	1	12	5	20	9	28	12
5	2	13	5	21	9	29	1
6	2	14	6	22	10	30	1
7	3	15	6	23	10	31	2
8	3	16	7	24	10		

Zodiacal Glyphs

♈	Aries
♉	Taurus
♊	Gemini
♋	Cancer
♌	Leo
♍	Virgo
♎	Libra
♏	Scorpio
♐	Sagittarius
♑	Capricorn
♒	Aquarius
♓	Pisces

	1923	1924	1925	1926	1927	1928	1929	1930	1931	1932	1933	1934	1935
JAN	♊	♏	♈	♌	♐	♈	♍	♑	♉	♎	♓	♋	♏
FEB	♌	♐	♉	♍	♑	♊	♏	♓	♋	♐	♈	♌	♑
MAR	♌	♑	♉	♍	♒	♋	♏	♓	♋	♐	♉	♍	♑
APR	♎	♓	♋	♏	♈	♍	♑	♉	♍	♒	♊	♎	♓
MAY	♏	♈	♌	♐	♉	♎	♒	♊	♎	♓	♋	♐	♈
JUN	♑	♉	♍	♒	♋	♏	♓	♌	♐	♉	♍	♑	♊
JUL	♒	♋	♏	♓	♌	♐	♈	♍	♑	♊	♎	♓	♋
AUG	♈	♌	♐	♉	♍	♒	♊	♏	♓	♋	♐	♈	♌
SEP	♉	♎	♒	♋	♌	♓	♌	♐	♈	♍	♑	♊	♎
OCT	♊	♏	♓	♌	♐	♉	♍	♑	♉	♎	♓	♋	♏
NOV	♌	♑	♉	♍	♑	♊	♏	♓	♋	♐	♈	♌	♑
DEC	♍	♒	♊	♎	♓	♌	♐	♈	♌	♑	♉	♍	♒

	1936	1937	1938	1939	1940	1941	1942	1943	1944	1945	1946	1947	1948
JAN	♈	♌	♑	♉	♍	♒	♊	♎	♓	♌	♐	♈	♍
FEB	♉	♎	♒	♊	♏	♈	♌	♐	♉	♍	♑	♊	♎
MAR	♊	♎	♒	♋	♐	♈	♌	♐	♉	♎	♒	♊	♏
APR	♌	♐	♈	♌	♑	♉	♎	♒	♋	♏	♓	♌	♑
MAY	♍	♑	♉	♎	♒	♊	♏	♓	♌	♐	♉	♍	♒
JUN	♎	♒	♋	♏	♈	♌	♑	♉	♎	♒	♊	♏	♓
JUL	♏	♈	♌	♑	♉	♍	♒	♊	♏	♓	♌	♐	♈
AUG	♑	♉	♎	♒	♋	♏	♈	♌	♐	♉	♍	♑	♊
SEP	♓	♋	♏	♈	♌	♑	♉	♍	♒	♋	♏	♓	♌
OCT	♈	♌	♑	♉	♎	♒	♊	♎	♋	♌	♐	♈	♍
NOV	♊	♎	♒	♊	♏	♈	♌	♐	♉	♍	♑	♊	♏
DEC	♋	♏	♓	♌	♑	♉	♍	♑	♊	♎	♒	♋	♐

	1949	1950	1951	1952	1953	1954	1955	1956	1957	1958	1959	1960	1961
JAN	♑	♊	♎	♓	♋	♏	♈	♌	♑	♉	♍	♒	♋
FEB	♓	♋	♐	♈	♍	♑	♉	♎	♒	♊	♏	♈	♌
MAR	♓	♋	♐	♉	♍	♑	♊	♏	♓	♋	♏	♈	♌
APR	♉	♍	♒	♊	♎	♓	♋	♐	♈	♌	♑	♊	♎
MAY	♊	♎	♓	♋	♐	♈	♍	♑	♉	♎	♒	♋	♏
JUN	♌	♐	♈	♍	♑	♊	♎	♓	♋	♐	♈	♌	♑
JUL	♍	♑	♊	♎	♓	♋	♏	♈	♌	♑	♉	♍	♒
AUG	♏	♓	♋	♐	♈	♍	♑	♉	♎	♒	♊	♏	♈
SEP	♐	♈	♍	♑	♊	♎	♒	♋	♐	♈	♌	♑	♊
OCT	♑	♊	♎	♓	♋	♏	♓	♌	♑	♉	♍	♒	♋
NOV	♓	♋	♏	♈	♍	♑	♉	♎	♒	♊	♏	♈	♌
DEC	♈	♌	♑	♊	♎	♒	♊	♏	♓	♌	♐	♉	♍

	1962	1963	1964	1965	1966	1967	1968	1969	1970	1971	1972	1973	1974
JAN	♏	♓	♌	♐	♈	♍	♑	♊	♎	♒	♋	♐	♈
FEB	♐	♉	♍	♒	♊	♏	♓	♋	♏	♈	♍	♑	♉
MAR	♐	♉	♎	♒	♊	♏	♈	♌	♐	♉	♍	♑	♊
APR	♒	♋	♏	♈	♌	♑	♉	♍	♒	♊	♏	♓	♋
MAY	♓	♌	♐	♉	♍	♒	♊	♎	♓	♋	♐	♈	♍
JUN	♉	♎	♒	♊	♏	♓	♌	♐	♉	♍	♑	♊	♎
JUL	♊	♏	♓	♌	♐	♈	♍	♑	♊	♎	♓	♋	♐
AUG	♌	♐	♉	♎	♒	♊	♏	♓	♋	♏	♈	♍	♑
SEP	♍	♒	♋	♏	♓	♋	♐	♉	♍	♑	♊	♎	♓
OCT	♏	♓	♌	♐	♈	♍	♒	♊	♎	♒	♋	♐	♈
NOV	♐	♉	♎	♒	♊	♎	♓	♋	♐	♈	♍	♑	♉
DEC	♑	♊	♏	♓	♋	♐	♈	♌	♐	♑	♎	♒	♊

	1975	1976	1977	1978	1979	1980	1981	1982	1983	1984	1985	1986	1987
JAN	♌	♑	♉	♍	♒	♊	♏	♓	♌	♐	♉	♍	♑
FEB	♎	♒	♋	♏	♈	♌	♐	♉	♍	♒	♊	♎	♓
MAR	♎	♓	♋	♏	♈	♍	♑	♉	♎	♒	♊	♏	♓
APR	♐	♈	♍	♑	♊	♎	♒	♋	♏	♈	♌	♑	♉
MAY	♑	♉	♎	♒	♋	♏	♓	♌	♐	♉	♍	♒	♊
JUN	♓	♋	♐	♈	♌	♑	♉	♎	♒	♊	♏	♓	♌
JUL	♈	♌	♑	♉	♍	♒	♋	♏	♓	♌	♐	♉	♍
AUG	♉	♎	♓	♋	♏	♈	♌	♐	♈	♎	♒	♊	♎
SEP	♋	♐	♈	♌	♐	♊	♎	♒	♊	♏	♓	♌	♐
OCT	♌	♑	♉	♍	♒	♋	♏	♓	♋	♐	♉	♍	♑
NOV	♎	♓	♋	♏	♓	♌	♐	♉	♍	♒	♊	♎	♓
DEC	♏	♈	♌	♐	♉	♍	♑	♊	♎	♓	♋	♐	♈

	1988	1989	1990	1991	1992	1993	1994	1995	1996	1997	1998	1999	2000
JAN	♊	♎	♒	♋	♏	♈	♌	♑	♉	♎	♒	♊	♏
FEB	♋	♐	♈	♍	♑	♉	♎	♒	♋	♏	♈	♌	♐
MAR	♌	♐	♉	♍	♒	♊	♎	♓	♋	♏	♈	♌	♑
APR	♍	♒	♊	♏	♓	♋	♐	♈	♍	♑	♊	♎	♓
MAY	♏	♓	♌	♐	♈	♍	♑	♉	♎	♒	♋	♏	♈
JUN	♐	♉	♍	♑	♊	♎	♓	♋	♐	♈	♌	♑	♉
JUL	♑	♊	♎	♒	♋	♐	♈	♌	♑	♉	♎	♒	♋
AUG	♓	♌	♐	♈	♍	♑	♉	♎	♓	♋	♏	♓	♌
SEP	♉	♍	♑	♊	♏	♓	♋	♏	♈	♌	♐	♉	♎
OCT	♊	♎	♒	♋	♐	♈	♌	♑	♉	♎	♒	♊	♏
NOV	♌	♐	♈	♍	♑	♉	♎	♒	♋	♏	♈	♌	♑
DEC	♍	♑	♉	♎	♒	♋	♏	♈	♌	♐	♉	♍	♒

THE
SOLAR SYSTEM

THE STARS, OTHER THAN THE SUN, PLAY NO PART IN THE SCIENCE OF ASTROLOGY. ASTROLOGERS USE ONLY THE BODIES IN THE SOLAR SYSTEM, EXCLUDING THE EARTH, TO CALCULATE HOW OUR LIVES AND PERSONALITIES CHANGE.

Pluto
Pluto takes 246 years to travel around the Sun. It affects our unconscious instincts and urges, gives us strength in difficulty, and perhaps emphasizes any inherent cruel streak.

Neptune
Neptune stays in each sign for 14 years. At best it makes us sensitive and imaginative; at worst it encourages deceit and carelessness, making us worry.

Uranus
Uranus's influence can make us friendly, kind, eccentric, inventive, and unpredictable.

Saturn
In ancient times, Saturn was the most distant known planet. Its influence can limit our ambition and make us either overly cautious (but practical), or reliable and self-disciplined.

SATURN

PLUTO

NEPTUNE

URANUS

Jupiter

Jupiter encourages expansion, optimism, generosity, and breadth of vision. It can, however, also make us wasteful, extravagant, and conceited.

Mars

Much associated with energy, anger, violence, selfishness, and a strong sex drive, Mars also encourages decisiveness and leadership.

JUPITER

Earth

Every planet contributes to the environment of the Solar System, and a person born on Venus would no doubt be influenced by our own planet in some way.

The Moon

Although it is a satelite of the Earth, the Moon is known in astrology as a planet. It lies about 240,000 miles from the Earth and, astrologically, is second in importance to the Sun.

MERCURY

THE MOON

VENUS

EARTH

MARS

The Sun

The Sun, the only star used by astrologers, influences the way we present ourselves to the world – our image or personality; the "us" we show to other people.

Venus

The planet of love and partnership, Venus can emphasize all our best personal qualities. It may also encourage us to be lazy, impractical, and too dependent on other people.

Mercury

The planet closest to the Sun affects our intellect. It can make us inquisitive, versatile, argumentative, perceptive, and clever, but maybe also inconsistent, cynical, and sarcastic.